JOURNEY TO BETHLEHEM

THE CHRISTMAS STORY THROUGH THE EYES OF THE BARE-FOOT PASTOR

REV. DEBBIE DROST

JOURNEY TO BETHLEHEM

*The Christmas Story through
the eyes of the "Bare-Foot Pastor"*

By

Rev. Debbie Drost

INTRODUCTION

A note to my husband:

It's that time of year that the house is a mess
Cleaning and cooking become less and less
Clothes pile up, and dinner is late
But the Hallmark channel and I have a date

It's only November, he says with a huff
What happened to Turkey, dressing, and stuff?
Football, dinner and a long afternoon nap?
I am not ready for "mamma in her kerchief and I in my cap!"

I tell him don't be so grumpy, you're not at your best
Go to your room and take a rest
'Tis the season to be Jolly, I say with a smile
Oh, and don't use the credit card for a while!

Does your house sound like my house in November, or maybe even earlier?

I love the Christmas season, walking in stores full of Christmas colors, and the smell of cinnamon and apples everywhere.

Most of the time, we don't even realize they are playing Christmas music until we are singing along with the little people in the speakers.

The world could sure use more words like Love, Joy, Peace, and Hope. These words always take center stage during the Christmas season.

Our loving God brought these words to flesh over 2,000 years ago.

Hallmark does not hold a candle to the Love stories found in the first Christmas story.

The Love between Zechariah and Elizabeth (parents of John the Baptist).
The Love between Joseph and Mary.
The Love for God from Joseph and Mary.
The Love of God for all of you.

Join me as we travel back in time to the first Christmas. Experience it all through the eyes of the barefoot pastor, and as God so lovingly allows me, "in the Revdeb version."

THE BIRTH OF JOHN

Let's begin this story with the full scripture taken from Luke 1: 5-25.

After you read the complete scripture, I will break it down for you in my "Revdeb version."

The Birth of John the Baptist Foretold
(NIV translation)

⁵ In the time of Herod king of Judea there was a priest named Zechariah, who belonged to the priestly division of Abijah; his wife Elizabeth was also a descendant of Aaron. ⁶ Both of them were righteous in the sight of God, observing all the Lord's commands and decrees blamelessly. ⁷ But they were childless because Elizabeth was not able to conceive, and they were both very old.

⁸ Once when Zechariah's division was on duty and he was serving as priest before God, ⁹ he was chosen by lot, according to the custom of the priesthood, to go into the temple of the Lord and burn incense. ¹⁰ And when the time for the burning of incense came, all the assembled worshipers were praying outside.

[11] Then an angel of the Lord appeared to him, standing at the right side of the altar of incense. [12] When Zechariah saw him, he was startled and was gripped with fear. [13] But the angel said to him: "Do not be afraid, Zechariah; your prayer has been heard. Your wife Elizabeth will bear you a son, and you are to call him John.

[14] He will be a joy and delight to you, and many will rejoice because of his birth, [15] for he will be great in the sight of the Lord. He is never to take wine or other fermented drink, and he will be filled with the Holy Spirit even before he is born. [16] He will bring back many of the people of Israel to the Lord their God.

[17] And he will go on before the Lord, in the spirit and power of Elijah, to turn the hearts of the parents to their children and the disobedient to the wisdom of the righteous—to make ready a people prepared for the Lord."

[18] Zechariah asked the angel, "How can I be sure of this? I am an old man and my wife is well along in years."

[19] The angel said to him, "I am Gabriel. I stand in the presence of God, and I have been sent to speak to you and to tell you this good news. [20] And now you will be silent and not able to speak until the day this happens, because you did not believe my words, which will come true at their appointed time."

[21] Meanwhile, the people were waiting for Zechariah and wondering why he stayed so long in the temple. [22] When he came out, he could not speak to them. They realized he had seen a vision in the temple, for he kept making signs to them but remained unable to speak.

[23] When his time of service was completed, he returned home. [24] After this his wife Elizabeth became pregnant and for five months remained in

seclusion. ²⁵ *"The Lord has done this for me," she said. "In these days he has shown his favor and taken away my disgrace among the people."*

~

Now, get comfortable, and let's get into the story.

Luke 1

⁵ *In the time of Herod king of Judea there was a priest named Zechariah, who belonged to the priestly division of Abijah; his wife Elizabeth was also a descendant of Aaron.*

⁶ *Both of them were righteous in the sight of God, observing all the Lord's commands and decrees blamelessly. ⁷ But they were childless because Elizabeth was not able to conceive, and they were both very old.*

Some of you might be a little surprised that the story of the Virgin Birth of Jesus starts off with the announcement about his cousin, John the Baptist.

Remember that John the Baptist is the forerunner of Jesus. He was born "to make a way for Jesus." John was born about six months before Jesus. Sit back, grab a drink (coffee please for me), and enjoy the story of Zechariah and Elizabeth.

It is amazing to me that a few short sentences, in the middle of a paragraph, can tell you so much about two people.

They both grew up in priestly homes. Zechariah went on to become what was expected of him, and I am sure he was proud to be called a priest. Elizabeth, having grown up in a priestly household, probably made an excellent "Preacher's wife."

How many of us would love to be recorded in the Bible as being "righteous in the sight of God"? You would think that if they carried that label, life would be clear skies and bright rainbows. The one word in verse 7 lets you know it does not work that way.

But...

3

Being childless in that time was a burden almost too heavy to bear. A woman's worth was all wrapped up in her being able to bear children, especially boys.

I wonder how many times Elizabeth cried herself to sleep at night? How many times Zechariah had to tell her it didn't matter because he loved her beyond any child she could carry.

How do you know this is true? There is no concubine for Zechariah. No other wives that could have borne him children. There is only Elizabeth. That was his choice. He had every right (legally) to do whatever he needed to, so he could have an heir. He chose his love for Elizabeth after his love for God.

How many times did they fall to their knees and pray to their God (the same as ours by the way), that he would bless them with a child of their own, only to be met with silence year after year?

I can sympathize with Elizabeth. When I was first married to Clayton, my first husband, the only thing I ever wanted to be was a good mom. It must have had something to do with growing up with so many siblings and getting to play "mom" every once in a while for them.

I have five brothers and one sister. I grew up in a big family, and I wanted to continue that tradition, but that wasn't God's plan for me. Every year of my marriage, Clayton and I tried for a little one, only to turn up empty.

Not just emptiness, but with a miscarriage every year for seven years. I never gave up though, and in that seventh year, we were blessed with a healthy baby girl.

Check out the last part of verse 7. "And" they were very old. They were done praying for a child. Their time had come and gone with no blessing in that area. I can't help but think they'd probably given up on getting that blessing from God. Much like Clayton and I had.

It's a good thing God has a plan and never gives up. Even in the midst of our doubt, He's faithful. He knew my heart, just as he knew Elizabeth's heart all those years ago. (And He knows yours too!)

Top off your drink and let's move further into the story. It's just getting good...

Luke 1: 8-10 ⁸ Once when Zechariah's division was on duty and he was serving as priest before God, ⁹ he was chosen by lot, according to the custom of the priesthood, to go into the temple of the Lord and burn incense. ¹⁰ And when the time for the burning of incense came, all the assembled worshipers were praying outside.

For Zechariah, being chosen to go into the temple and burn incense for his people was like any of us winning the lottery.

There were somewhere around twenty-thousand priests in and around Judea at that time. They were divided into twenty-four sections. Zechariah served in the eighth section of Abijah. Each section served in the Temple twice a year for one week at a time.

Because there were so many priests in the section, the duties were assigned by lot. Lots could be sticks with markings, stones with symbols, etc., which were thrown into a small area and then the result was interpreted. (1)

Revdeb version: this is a lot like our "rolling of the dice."

As Zechariah went into the area where he would burn the incense for his people, scripture says everyone else was outside praying.

I love thinking about Elizabeth being so proud of her Zechariah. This was a once in a lifetime event. Zechariah had been with the division of Abijah all his life. Remember, he is "old" now. Not once in all those years had he been chosen.

Today – He walked into the Temple because God breathed onto the stones that they tossed out to see who would go!

～

Luke 1:11-13a
   ¹¹ Then an angel of the Lord appeared to him, standing at the right

side of the altar of incense. [12] *When Zechariah saw him, he was startled and was gripped with fear.* [13 a)] *But the angel said to him: "Do not be afraid, Zechariah; your prayer has been heard."*

Picture this: Zechariah coming into the room for the first time. In awe of the Holy presence of the place. (Jaw dropping). I am sure he would love to just stand and absorb this feeling for a while, but he really is there for a specific reason, and he knows he needs to move on with his task.

He lights the incense and begins to lift up the prayers that have been recited by the Jewish community for thousands of years.

As he gets into it, he senses the presence of someone beside him. I compare this to that moment in the movies when the girl should have gotten out of the house before the phone rang!

For a few seconds, which probably seems longer to Zechariah, he keeps his eyes closed thinking "no one should be in here with me, it's my turn!" O.K., maybe that would be my thought.

[12] *"When Zechariah saw him, he was startled and gripped with fear."*

This is one of those moments when you read scripture and go "Duh!" Who wouldn't be?

God is so good, though, and He has taught his Angels well. Angel 101 – Learn to repeat, *"Do Not Be Afraid."* An Angel cannot move to the next section of learning until he can repeat this phrase without laughing. (Revdeb version!)

Here is one of my favorite verses in this story. I have broken it apart so you can get the human side of Zechariah (and me).

Luke 1: 13a (When you see a scripture like this, it means they are giving you the first part of the sentence.)

13a But the angel said to him: "Do not be afraid, Zechariah; your prayer has been heard."

Here is the Rev Deb version:

"Wow, really? I just got here. The first time I come in, and it's MY prayers that have been heard?"

"Wait, What prayers? Or better yet... which prayers?"

13b "Your wife Elizabeth will bear you a son, and you are to call him John."

Do you think Zechariah heard anything after that? Was the lighting in this part of the Temple so bad that maybe the Angel landed in the wrong place? Did the stones lie? Was someone much younger supposed to be in here? I know he could not be referring to me and my wife! Wait – He did say "your wife Elizabeth."

Better tune back in, Zechariah, for the rest of the message.

∽

Luke 1 14-17
14 "He will be a joy and delight to you, and many will rejoice because of his birth, 15 for he will be great in the sight of the Lord. He is never to take wine or other fermented drink, and he will be filled with the Holy Spirit even before he is born.

16 He will bring back many of the people of Israel to the Lord their God. 17 And he will go on before the Lord, in the spirit and power of Elijah, to turn the hearts of the parents to their children and the disobedient to the wisdom of the righteous—to make ready a people prepared for the Lord."

This, my friends, is why John the Baptist had to have his birth story first. He was only six months older, but his ministry was already laid out for him. His ministry was *to make ready a people prepared for the Lord*.

What parent wouldn't want to hear those words about the birth of their son or daughter? Don't jump on the wish wagon yet though. John the Baptist had a tough life as you will see when the Easter Book comes out.

You've got to love Zechariah's next words. Really, this would so be me.

Luke 1: 18
¹⁸ Zechariah asked the angel, "How can I be sure of this? I am an old man and my wife is well along in years."

I would be okay with Roy (my husband of 32 years) calling himself old. I am not sure how *strongly* I would react to him talking about me being "well along in years."

It is a good argument for Zechariah. Those prayers have long been silenced.

So many of you reading this have had encounters with Jesus, or an Angel sent by Jesus. Like Zechariah, you have doubted the truth and reality of that encounter. You have shoved the event into a recessed part of your heart and let the enemy make you believe that it did not happen or was just a crazy dream. Don't let the enemy rob you of your miracle.

I don't think the Angel, who just recited a powerful message to Zechariah, was very happy with Zechariah's doubt.

Luke 1: 18
¹⁹ The angel said to him, "I am Gabriel. I stand in the presence of God, and I have been sent to speak to you and to tell you this good news."

There are many ways, I guess, that you could hear these words from Gabriel. Since I am writing the book, I get to tell you how I hear them.

In a big booming voice of a ticked off Angel!

"I AM GABRIEL!!! I stand in the presence of God, and I have been sent to speak to you and to tell you this good news."

Revdeb Version:

"How dare you not believe! Do YOU stand in the presence of God every day? Well, I DO! Do you know who sent me to speak to you? That's right little man, unbeliever, GOD DID!! This was GOOD NEWS!"

Chill Gabriel. Zechariah only asked a simple question. The question today would throw any case out of court.

Gabriel was having none of it though. He was large and in charge. He was judge and jury. Then he passed down the sentence for the doubt Zechariah voiced.

Luke 1:20

²⁰ "And now you will be silent and not able to speak until the day this happens, because you did not believe my words, which will come true at their appointed time."

And the gavel slams down.

Case dismissed.

Zechariah will have to learn sign language fast. Where's Google and YouTube when you need them?

Gabriel does give him a timeline though if you look back at the scripture. He tells him he will remain silent "until the day this happens."

I wonder if all this has messed with Zechariah's mind? Does he think "What happens? Oh, the part where us old people are going to have a baby in our old age?"

Did he do the math of how long Sarah had to wait after she was told she was going to have a child? Ten years? That is a long time to be silent.

When I think about ten years of Roy (my hubs) being silent – hmmm???

Time to go Zechariah. Time to walk back out to all those people that have been on their knees praying outside while you were being blessed and reprimanded in the Temple.

Luke 1:21
   ²¹ Meanwhile, the people were waiting for Zechariah and wondering why he stayed so long in the temple.

~

Let's slip into Elizabeth's sandals for a few moments.

We last left her feeling very proud of her Zechariah. He had been chosen to represent his people. She watched him walk into the temple with his head held high.

Now, she along with a thousand more people started to get worried. It should not be taking this long. Something has gone wrong in there. Did he have a heart attack? Was he so wrapped up in the Holiness of the place that he forgot he could not live there?

She could hear the rumbling of the others wondering the same thoughts she was having.

Do you not find it amazing how we can go from the mountaintop experience to the valley in a matter of minutes? I believe Elizabeth was in this place as she waited for her husband to come out of the Temple.

Luke 1:22

²² When he came out, he could not speak to them. They realized he had seen a vision in the temple, for he kept making signs to them but remained unable to speak.

Have you ever watched the movie *The Ten Commandments* with Charlton Heston? O.K. A more real question would be "Have you NOT watched the movie *The Ten Commandments* starring Charlton Heston?"

I have seen it more times than I care to admit. I've said it many times in my life, but it's the truth. If Moses doesn't look like Charlton Heston when I get to Heaven, (yes, I am definitely going) then I won't recognize him (Moses).

Since we're on the subject of the movie...

There is a scene where Moses goes up to the burning bush, and God talks to him for a while.

When he is returning to the valley, his physical appearance has completely changed.

The first thing his wife (in the movie) says, "He has seen the Lord."

I tell you this because when Zechariah comes out of the Temple, everyone knows something happened. It's visibly obvious.

Maybe his whole appearance didn't change much since it was an Angel and not God he encountered, but it was enough that people knew he had seen a vision. Maybe his eyes were wide, maybe his mouth slack... something was up.

Can you feel the stress rolling off Elizabeth as she sees her husband come out of the temple? He is alive.

Wait for it —

"Why is he not saying anything? Why is he looking at me so funny?"

Well, Elizabeth, your world is fixing to be rocked!

Age means absolutely nothing to our God. He is timeless, and a thousand years to us could quite simply be a moment to Him. It's a mystery, and a beautiful one at that.

Luke 1: 23-25
²³ When his time of service was completed, he returned home. ²⁴ After this his wife Elizabeth became pregnant and for five months remained in seclusion. ²⁵ "The Lord has done this for me," she said. "In these days he has shown his favor and taken away my disgrace among the people."

Zechariah and Elizabeth did not live in Jerusalem. They lived in the Hills of Judea. Hebron to be exact. It was about forty miles (give or take a few miles) between Hebron and Jerusalem.

Scripture says that for five months Elizabeth remained in seclusion. She did not return to the Temple when Zechariah did.

Do you wonder why she remained in seclusion? If we look at it in our shoes today, there are several reasons I can relate to it.

First, after five miscarriages for me, I stopped telling people I was pregnant. I thought if I did not say it out loud, maybe this pregnancy would stick. Maybe I'd have a chance at having a baby.

Second, you really don't want to see the sympathy on people's faces for the fifth or sixth time. It gets so old being the one they're all thinking "poor thing" about.

If you think about the time you heard on the news that a sixty-year-old woman was pregnant, combine that with about ten or more years for Elizabeth. Not only that, but she was pregnant for the first time.

Yeah, I get the seclusion part for Elizabeth. The one thing she does that many of us forget to do, is to give praise to God for giving her the one thing her heart has always yearned for.

A Child. A Son.

The second thing God has done for her?

Luke 1: 25b "taken away my disgrace among the people."

You may have not realized it at the beginning of this book, but Elizabeth lived every day, every hour, every minute with the disgrace. Not just because the town pressed that on her for her barrenness, but she lived with it inside her own soul. Remember the time we were in when this narrative was played out. Women's worth relied on their ability to have children and in particular – sons.

It might be hard for some reading this to understand why Elizabeth felt this disgrace. You would have to research the Jewish beliefs and way of life so long ago. Even then, it is hard for a 21st-century Woman to accept.

For some of you reading this, it's not so hard to understand. The desire, soul-crushing want, to have a child. Today, God gives us many different ways to be a parent. There are many kiddos out there waiting to be adopted, loved, warm and fed.

We are leaving Zechariah and Elizabeth now.

We will return to them at the end of the book. Check out the rest of the story for more on our priestly couple who experience a combination of miracles while living out their daily lives faithfully.

For now... we're heading over to Nazareth.

Come on. Let's go!

THE BIRTH OF JESUS FORETOLD

Let's read together the story of Mary's encounter with the Angel Gabriel from Luke 1: 26-38.

²⁶ In the sixth month of Elizabeth's pregnancy, God sent the angel Gabriel to Nazareth, a town in Galilee, ²⁷ to a virgin pledged to be married to a man named Joseph, a descendant of David. The virgin's name was Mary. ²⁸ The angel went to her and said, "Greetings, you who are highly favored! The Lord is with you."

²⁹ Mary was greatly troubled at his words and wondered what kind of greeting this might be. ³⁰ But the angel said to her, "Do not be afraid, Mary; you have found favor with God.

³¹ You will conceive and give birth to a son, and you are to call him Jesus. ³² He will be great and will be called the Son of the Most High. The Lord God will give him the throne of his father David, ³³ and he will reign over Jacob's descendants forever; his kingdom will never end."

³⁴ "How will this be," Mary asked the angel, "since I am a virgin?"

³⁵ The angel answered, "The Holy Spirit will come on you, and the power of the Most High will overshadow you. So the holy one to be born will be called[b] the Son of God. ³⁶ Even Elizabeth your relative is going to have a child in her old age, and she who was said to be unable to conceive is in her sixth month. ³⁷ For no word from God will ever fail."

³⁸ "I am the Lord's servant," Mary answered. "May your word to me be fulfilled." Then the angel left her.

I would like to start this section by telling you that sometimes the conversation Jesus has with us *is only with* us.

Before any discussion with Joseph, Mary's parents, or Elizabeth, Jesus comes to Mary alone.

Sometimes it is a lonely road He puts us on. I believe, in the story of Mary, she had to say "yes" before any other discussions would come to be.

As you slip on Mary's sandals, be aware, this young woman was only thirteen years old. Research shows she was somewhere between twelve and fourteen, so thirteen seems pretty safe.

I know you are reading this and probably looking at your own daughter or granddaughter and thinking, "no way!" Please be careful not to bring your 2017 lifestyle into a story that took place over 2,000 years ago. Things were much different in those days and with the Jewish culture. But one thing remained the same, Mary was a young, innocent girl. Don't take that from her when you close your eyes and walk through this beautiful story – emotions and all!

Wait. Open your eyes. How in the world are you going to read with them closed? (Some of you will have a quip for that. Good for you. I love it.)

Now, let's join Mary and Gabriel in the backyard (Revdeb Version).

First, Scripture gives us an idea of the timing of this visit to Mary. Check it out.

Luke 1:26a
> *²⁶ In the sixth month of Elizabeth's pregnancy,*

Remember where we left Elizabeth? If not, just turn back to the last page. She is home in the hills of Judea, in seclusion. She will soon play a huge part in this conversation between Mary and Gabriel. *Wait for it....*

Luke 1: 26-27
> *²⁶ In the sixth month of Elizabeth's pregnancy, God sent the angel Gabriel to Nazareth, a town in Galilee, ²⁷ to a virgin pledged to be married to a man named Joseph, a descendant of David. The virgin's name was Mary.*

Look how much information God has given us in just two verses of Scripture.

First (after the information about Elizabeth), Gabriel lets us know exactly who sent Gabriel.

God did.

Second, He lets us know the exact location of where Mary is.

Nazareth, a town in Galilee.

Third, more important than her name is her physical status.

A virgin pledged to be married.

Next, who she is pledged to.

A man named Joseph.

More important than His name is his ancestry.

A descendant of David.

NOW – We get to know her name.

The virgin's name was Mary!

That, my friend, is a lot of information and how scripture works most of the time. If you take the time to read it completely, every word, it **will** revel mighty wonders you passed over the first time.

O.K. Here you are in the backyard, doing whatever it is a thirteen-year-old girl did in those days. Suddenly, an Angel is standing there beside you. Gabriel must have been a stunning vision to behold.

Luke 1:2

The angel went to her and said, "Greetings, you who are highly favored! The Lord is with you."

How long do you think it took Mary to realize this vision of an angel spoke to her? For me? I would still have that "deer in the headlights" look!

What powerful words for a thirteen-year-old girl to hear from an angel standing in her backyard.

I can just see Mary looking around wondering if anyone else is seeing what she sees. We know there is no one else seeing this. Gabriel has made sure that this conversation is only being heard and spoken between them.

Mary has been raised in a Godly home. From the time she was born, she has heard the stories told through the ages repeatedly.

Mary probably understands the second part of Gabriel's words. *"The Lord is with you."* It is the *"highly favored"* part she is having trouble understanding.

Luke 1: 28

²⁹ Mary was greatly troubled at his words and wondered what kind of greeting this might be.

Wouldn't you be *greatly troubled* with those words if you suddenly heard them in your heart? Hey, Debbie (Laura, Lois, Beth – insert your name here), *"You are highly favored by God."*

"Why me? I am a nobody, Lord. I am unworthy of being **highly favored.** I'm what one might call a 'hot mess.'"

No matter how many years pass, some things will never change.

We know how Zechariah handled seeing Gabriel; let's see how Mary deals with it.

Luke 1:30
30 But the angel said to her, "Do not be afraid, Mary; you have found favor with God."

Oh, O.K. Don't be afraid. (Yeah right.)

An Angel standing in my backyard is no reason to be afraid? (Surely, I'm being punked.)

I've found favor with God? (No way. That's it. The end is near.)

Just in case – If I ask him to explain, will I need to learn sign language too?

And then the Ball drops!

Luke 1: 31-33
31 "You will conceive and give birth to a son, and you are to call him Jesus. 32 He will be great and will be called the Son of the Most High. The Lord God will give him the throne of his father David, 33 and he will reign over Jacob's descendants forever; his kingdom will never end."

Mary is probably thinking the "highly favored" part was easier to understand than the rest of his announcement.

When you look back at the words Gabriel spoke to Zechariah about his son, John, and what he would be like, he is basically telling

Mary the same think about her son. Not in exactly the same words, but he is telling them both what to expect out of their sons.

Mary is told that her son will be the Son of God. He will fulfill the prophecy of coming from the line of David. Mary, as I said before, had heard these stories from the old prophets passed down many times. I can imagine she never thought she would hear them from a messenger of God spoken directly to her.

As you see in the next verse, she catches the first part of the announcement.

Luke 1:34
³⁴ "How will this be," Mary asked the angel, "since I am a virgin?"

Remember from the first part of Mary's story, she is already engaged to Joseph. This might be a good time to tell you a little bit about the Jewish custom of engagement. Seems fitting to insert that right on in!

In those times, Jewish marriages were arranged by the parents. It was similar to a contract between two families more than anything else.

Today, engagements turn out to be only a wee bit smaller than a wedding.

My granddaughter, Katelyn, got engaged a few months ago. Michael, her intended, planned it all out.

There were about ten to fifteen people involved with the plan. His best friends were strategically placed with video equipment. Dinner was set, and the location was scouted out perfectly.

Family was home decorating the house. Food was being prepared and set out. Phones were charged and waiting for the ding to announce she said YES!

Finally, they were back to the house with friends and family shouting Congratulations!! Hugs all around and a few tears. They grow up way too fast.

But Katie's present-day engagement was nothing like Mary's engagement 2,000 years ago.

Mary and Joseph were married in the eyes of everyone once the contract was signed by both parents.

The deal was that they could not be together for a year. There was no consummation of the marriage for that time. During the year, Mary would live at home with her parents and Joseph would begin working on a house for them to live together in when the year was complete.

So, when Mary asked Gabriel the question, it was a humble and honest question. She and Joseph had not been together, and according to the timeline, it would be another nine months at least before the year was up.

Maybe Mary wanted to make sure Gabriel knew she had not broken any laws. She made sure to tell him she was still a virgin. You know, just in case the shiny, bright angel needed help figuring out how babies are made. That would so be me!

It would seem that Gabriel was ready for the explanation.

Luke 1:35
35 The angel answered, "The Holy Spirit will come on you, and the power of the Most High will overshadow you. So the holy one to be born will be called[b] the Son of God."

I doubt Mary really understood what Gabriel was saying about the Holy Spirit. *The power of the Most High will overshadow you.* Mary probably knew that the "Most High" was God, and a peace came upon her thanks to that. No matter what, God is in charge, and whatever He wants or needs, she was all in. She trusted Him.

I remember when God called me into ministry. I had been cutting hair for almost eighteen years in Huntsville, Texas. Not only that, but I had been attending Sam Houston State University for twelve years (taking a course or two every semester, raising a family and working.)

Some of you feel like I'm telling your story in that last sentence, right?

I was in my last semester at SHSU, only a few weeks from graduating with a health education degree.

I knew God was calling me to follow him, I just didn't know what that looked like. My plea bargaining with God had gotten me nowhere. I would let him know my answer when He showed me what He wanted me to do. Has that really worked for anyone since time began? Yeah, well, it didn't work for me either.

Finally, one day, after many days of bargains, I was cutting a young man's hair, and I could not take God's silence any longer.

I threw up my hands and said, "FINE, WHATEVER YOU WANT, I WILL DO IT!"

"I really just wanted a plain haircut," said the startled young man in my chair.

He was completely unaware of the battle in my mind and heart to do what God wanted rather than me being in charge of my life.

It's funny now, but I am sure that young man thought I needed to be fitted for a straitjacket. He might not have been *too* far off from the truth.

I believe that's how Mary must have felt. It's overwhelming to hear God's plan for your life. It never seems to be what you had planned. I don't have to live 2,000 years ago to feel Mary's surrender.

I feel it every time God whispers, "Ready to go?"

But Mary had peace over the decision. How do we know that?

Check out the next verse.

Luke 1:38

38 "I am the Lord's servant," Mary answered. "May your word to me be fulfilled." Then the angel left her.

No matter what He asks of me, I am but a servant of the Most High God. Let it come, and let the pieces fall where they may.

~

Thoughts must have gone around and around in Mary's head later that night. If you have ever taken something that happened in the daylight and carried it through the night, you know it gets bigger and bigger the darker the night.

Mary must have relived that conversation in her mind a thousand times and in a thousand different ways. I think most of what came out of her thoughts were, "Did that really happen? It was only me that saw the Angel, that heard those words, so maybe it only happened in my head?"

God knew she would question herself the next day.

God knew she would wonder if any of that conversation took place.

He gave her one sentence in that whole conversation with Gabriel that she would find her answer in. Do you remember what the sentence was?

Think about it. We'll come right back to it. First, let me share my own story of "did that really happen?"

In the year 2002, I was asked to go on an Emmaus Walk, which is a fantastic retreat that's organized by the Upper Room Ministries. You can check it out by going to www.hnec.org.

I had already accepted the call into ministry from God. I really didn't know how I could learn anything more by going on a retreat but whatever! I went in obedience without understanding. We serve because we're called to serve, and oftentimes because of saying "yes" we're changed for the better.

My only request to God, as I was heading out to the retreat, was just to let me know that He was with me.

The Walk to Emmaus is a three-day retreat with many blessings. Most of those blessings are revealed along the three days, but never a moment too soon. I won't go into them because if you have not been, I don't want to spoil anything for you. I will only tell you what is relevant to this story.

The first night we were there, we saw a film about the disciples.

Then we went into the chapel before going to bed. The Spiritual Director (Pastor) of the walk gave a short devotional about closing our eyes and going to the place where we find God.

That was pretty easy for me. I always fancy myself as Julie Andrews in *The Sound of Music*. I'd be singing and dancing up the hill-side. When, in my dream vision, I got to the top of the hill where we (me and Julie) throw our arms out wide and spin, I got this over-whelming feeling I was no longer alone on that mountaintop.

I knew that if I turned around, I'd no longer be alone there, nor would I ever be the same again. It was a watershed moment for me.

Insert here that this is the part in the scary movie that the others are yelling, "Get out of the House!"

If I'm being completely honest, I was terrified to turn around. Change is never easy, and fear of the unknown is something we all share in common.

But I couldn't stand there any longer. I had to know if He was behind me.

As I turned around, there was Jesus. Standing there. He was dressed in His robe, and behind him looked like the open tomb. He never said a word. He just looked at me.

I know what scripture means about falling to your knees when in the presence of someone so Holy. I never gave it a thought. I just fell to my knees in front of Him.

When I did, I heard the Spiritual Director somewhere in the distance say, "O.K. Come back into the room now." I looked up, and everything looked the same in that little chapel.

The next thing the Spiritual Director said was, "and now we go into a time of silence. For the next twelve hours, do not talk to anyone. This silence is a chance for you to communicate with Jesus and center yourself for the next three days."

And then they sent us to our rooms.

I must tell you I was in a state of despair. This was the greatest thing I'd ever had happen to me, and I couldn't tell anyone. Are you kidding me?

I had a very long, restless night. Every time I closed my eyes, I could see Jesus standing there. Funny enough, I wasn't the only lady awake that night.

As you might guess, Satan spent all night twisting my belief in what I saw. By the time morning came, Satan had convinced me no one would believe me. No one ever sees Jesus. Especially someone as insignificant as me. Who would ever believe that I had asked Jesus to reveal himself to me this special weekend and He did? Me? An unworthy country girl from Mississippi? Please. As if...

It was much better if I just kept my mouth shut.

A little later after the silence was over, we formed a circle and sang a few songs. One of the songs was *I want to see you*. It really didn't matter if anyone else believed me, Jesus was still there when I closed my eyes. So that's what I did. I closed my eyes and sang to Jesus on top of the hill as He smiled at me.

As soon as the song ended, one of the retreat leaders, one I had not spoken to yet, tapped me on the shoulder, startling me.

I opened my eyes and looked at her.

"You see Him, don't you?" she asked.

"See who?"

She replied, "Jesus. You see his face, don't you?"

Here was the moment of truth for me. Did I answer as Satan had instructed me all through the night? Did I tell her the truth - yes, I see Jesus's face? Would they escort me off the walk silently, or would I go down screaming?

I looked at her for a moment and then a simple, "Yes, I see His face," came out of my heart and mouth.

Just like Zechariah, there must have been something about the look in my eyes or the expression on my face. Maybe I was a little more alive looking, but whatever it was, someone else could see it all over me. You cannot step in the presence of The Almighty and walk away unchanged.

There are so many of you reading this story right now, and I know you have had the same experience. I know Satan worked on you exactly how he worked on me. There is one thing Satan never quite gets though... God will give you something to grab onto that Satan cannot see. Something to verify or validate that yes, it did happen. You're not making it up.

What God gave me that night so long ago was the sweet voice of the retreat leader reminding me that I did see Jesus that night. What God gave Mary was a sentence to remember. Something to check it all out with.

Do you remember the sentence that Gabriel spoke to Mary? The sentence that helped her know that the entire conversation and all that it entailed was truly real?

Let me get it for you...

Luke 1:36-37
³⁶ "Even Elizabeth your relative is going to have a child in her old age, and she who was said to be unable to conceive is in her sixth month. ³⁷ For no word from God will ever fail."

Here, Gabriel is not only giving Mary something to hold on to when she doubts, but also, a reminder that the God she has heard about all her young life can do anything.

Mary wakes up and has convinced herself, like me, that no one would believe her. Maybe she could not even believe it happened.

"Wait a minute," she thinks, "what did the angel say about my cousin Elizabeth? Something about her being with child. Something about her already being in her sixth month?

"I must go to her. I must see if all of this is true. If Elizabeth is truly pregnant, then I will know that I not only have conceived but carry the Son of God."

Mary begins her journey from Nazareth to Judea.

MARY VISITS ELIZABETH

L et's continue the story...

Luke 1:39-40
³⁹ At that time Mary got ready and hurried to a town in the hill country of Judea, ⁴⁰ where she entered Zechariah's home and greeted Elizabeth.

The trip from Mary's home to the home of Zechariah and Elizabeth's is approximately sixty-five to seventy miles. It would have been a good journey for Mary, one I'm sure was worth it for Mary to have peace of mind.

Luke 1:41
⁴¹ When Elizabeth heard Mary's greeting, the baby leaped in her womb, and Elizabeth was filled with the Holy Spirit.

Picture the scene. Elizabeth sitting outside enjoying the warmth of the sun. Maybe she was working on a few *blue* baby clothes. One thing you can be sure of is there is a huge smile on the face of Elizabeth as she runs her hand over the large baby bump.

It takes a moment, but Elizabeth hears her name called. At the same time she hears her name spoken from Mary's lips, scripture says the **baby leaped in her womb.**

John *recognized* the Mother of his Lord. Pretty cool, huh?

Elizabeth recognized she was in the presence of a greater miracle that she had experienced. She was in the presence of the Lord.

Luke 1:42-44

In a loud voice she exclaimed: "Blessed are you among women, and blessed is the child you will bear! ⁴³ But why am I so favored, that the mother of my Lord should come to me? ⁴⁴ As soon as the sound of your greeting reached my ears, the baby in my womb leaped for joy."

If Mary needed assurance, she received it and more as she stood in front of Elizabeth. There was no doubting what Gabriel had said. Inside of her was a child. A Son. Her Son. The Son of God. The Redeemer she had heard about all her life.

Luke 1:45

⁴⁵ *"Blessed is she who has believed that the Lord would fulfill his promises to her!"*

Mary was truly blessed. God had chosen her to carry His Son, Jesus.

Don't you think that when God calls us to do something for Him that He would make the way easy?

Mary was surely blessed, but as she returns home, life will take a drastic turn for the "not so blessed." Mary's trials are about to take over her life. Maybe the next few months Mary is facing, as she travels back home, is one of the main reasons God chose her to be the Mother of Jesus.

We will have to head over to the book of Matthew to read the story of Joseph. Mark your place here in Luke though. We will be returning there after we walk with Joseph and Mary for a bit.

What are you waiting for? Come on... our journey isn't over just yet!

MARY AND JOSEPH

I want to begin by telling you the following story is a love story. It is one of the greatest romance stories ever written.

I am not just talking about the love God had for this world that He sent His only Son.

I am talking about two young people who live in the town of Nazareth, who are about to experience the ride of a lifetime.

You may have heard different ideas about the marriage of Mary and Joseph, but, this is the Revdeb version, and I can't help but put love as our number one theme.

Why?

I truly believe God would not choose an earthly family to have and raise his Son if there was not abundant love within the core of the marriage.

Was it an arranged marriage? Yes, arranged by God. Did Joseph really love Mary? With all his heart (scripture will testify to this in the following story.)

Did Mary love Joseph? I believe in today's term that she thought he was "HOT!" I really am a romantic at heart. Ignore that hot part…

I also believe that love began at the first look, but deepened as Mary and Joseph went through all they did together.

When Clayton (my first husband) and I were married in 1972, we both came from difficult home lives. We were young in age (17 and 19), but we were old in life. We both had a lot of home responsibilities that caused us to grow up too fast.

Getting married was really our way out of those lives. I did think he was "hot" though, and he thought I was perfect! Silly right? It's that initial attraction.

Real love, deep love, came after years of living life together. I always like to tell people Clayton and I grew young together. Maybe this is your story too.

I tell you this because most of you know the Christmas Advent Story. And I know most of you don't know the "Revdeb version" of the story. If I'm wrong, and you've heard me preach before, then you know life is about to turn rough for our young couple. You also know the hardship they are going to face together. In these tough times, then and now, love becomes real and deep. It's formed in the groves of living life together.

Let's slip off Mary's shoes now and tie on Joseph's sandals instead.

First, here is the Scripture from the Book of Matthew:

Matthew 1: 18-25
Joseph Accepts Jesus as His Son
¹⁸ This is how the birth of Jesus the Messiah came about: His mother Mary was pledged to be married to Joseph, but before they came together, she was found to be pregnant through the Holy Spirit.

¹⁹ Because Joseph her husband was faithful to the law, and yet did not want to expose her to public disgrace, he had in mind to divorce her quietly.

²⁰ But after he had considered this, an angel of the Lord appeared to him in a dream and said, "Joseph son of David, do not be afraid to take Mary home as your wife, because what is conceived in her is from the Holy Spirit. ²¹ She will give birth to a son, and you are to give him the name Jesus, because he will save his people from their sins."

²² All this took place to fulfill what the Lord had said through the prophet: ²³ "The virgin will conceive and give birth to a son, and they will call him Immanuel" (which means "God with us.")

²⁴ When Joseph woke up, he did what the angel of the Lord had commanded him and took Mary home as his wife. ²⁵ But he did not consummate their marriage until she gave birth to a son. And he gave him the name Jesus.

That is some tough reading, huh? It will make more sense and you will feel so much love through these verses as we break them apart and take it slow. Sometimes slowing down just a tad will open up something new you've yet to discover.

We know the first few verses because we just covered them in the Book of Luke when we were walking with Mary, but let's include it because every word from God is fruitful.

Matthew 1:18

¹⁸ This is how the birth of Jesus the Messiah came about: His mother Mary was pledged to be married to Joseph, but before they came together, she was found to be pregnant through the Holy Spirit.

Let me slip into Revdeb mode right now and tell the story.

Mary has just made her way back home. She spent some time with

Elizabeth and Zechariah before returning, which was nice, but probably not nearly long enough. But, it's time to go, and so she leaves. When she reaches the outskirts of Nazareth, her heart is beating fast, and she is feeling more than a little worried.

What will her family say when they see her? What will Joseph do? Will they believe her? How could they, when she hardly believed it herself? Even right now, looking down at her swollen belly and feeling the baby move inside her, she still has her moments.

She walks into the small town, and all eyes are on her. Smiles and happy laughter at seeing her have turned to shocked faces and disgusted looks.

Her parents stand in front of her with sadness and questioning looks. Only one word was spoken by her father. Her name. Mary.

Joseph hears Mary has returned and runs with all his might to hug the girl he loves, the woman he will spend the rest of his life with, doing everything he can to make her as happy as he is.

Joseph fights his way through the crowd and finally bursts out to come face to face with Mary.

Mary, a very pregnant Mary. Mary carrying a child that is not his.

Every dream, every smile, every ounce of happiness seeps out of Joseph.

He turns and walks back through the crowd and out of town in silence.

It is not long before a family meeting is called. Joseph, Mary's parents, and Joseph's parents are all in the room. Voices are getting louder and louder. No one is listening to each other.

Finally, Joseph yells for them to be quiet. He must know what happened. Who had Mary cheated on him with? Why would she cheat on him?

"Let Mary Speak," Joseph said.

Quiet filled the room. All eyes had turned to Mary as she kept one hand on her swollen belly.

Mary took a deep breath and began to tell the story of that visit from Gabriel. She told them how she was pregnant with the Son of God. She begged them to believe her, but no one did.

Joseph kept begging Mary to tell the truth, but Mary kept repeating that she was telling the truth.

Joseph gave Mary and her family one heartbreaking look before walking out the front door, the young man completely destroyed.

Mary's parents continued to beg her for the truth. They were fearful about the decision that Joseph had to make now. He could request the town stone his fiancé, and Mary's life would be over. Nothing could be more terrifying than sitting and waiting for resolution.

Mary's life hung in the balance, and the heartbroken man she loved was the one who would make the call. Live or die?

Let's slip back into scripture.

Matthew 1:19

¹⁹ Because Joseph her husband was faithful to the law, and yet did not want to expose her to public disgrace, he had in mind to divorce her quietly.

Joseph was a godly man. He was raised Jewish and upheld all the Jewish rules and customs. He would never think to break any of the laws that were written upon his mind and his heart.

Joseph knew Mary was with child. That much was undeniable. What was also obvious to Joseph was that the child was not his. He had not broken the sacred law of waiting the year before consummating his marriage to Mary. He would never do that. As he walked through the crowd the other day, it was clear that some of his best friends thought he had broken the sacred law.

How could Mary have done this to him? To them? The thoughts that must have been going through the town's people's heads were disturbing. It wasn't just her reputation at stake, but his as well.

The town was waiting for his decision. According to the Jewish laws, Joseph had to choose one of three options.

First: He had every right, and many expected him to choose this option, to have Mary stoned to death. The law stated that he could bring her out into the town square and have her stoned until no breath was left in her.

Second: He could claim the child as his and take Mary home as his wife.

Third: He could silently divorce her.

Let's break it down a little further. Joseph would not consider the first option, even though many of his friends encouraged him to.

Remember when I said this in the opening page of Mary and Joseph's story?

Was it an arranged marriage? Yes, arranged by God. Did Joseph really love Mary? With all his heart (scripture will testify to this in the following story.)

Here is how we know that he loved her with all his heart. First, his heart was breaking over this turn of events. Second, he chose not to have her stoned. He could not bring himself to have her die. Not many men in that time would have hesitated to go with option one.

The second option was not really one Joseph could choose either. Even though he loved her, he knew the child was not his. To take her home as his wife would allow everyone to believe that he had not followed God, which was a lie.

Notice the scripture says:

[19b] *"He had in mind to divorce her quietly."*

This tells us his decision was finally made, but he had not told Mary nor her parents yet. We then find out that after he made his decision, sleep came easier.

Isn't that true for all of us? We can toss and turn, back and forth, yes – no – maybe, all night. Once a decision is made, sleep will finally come.

Matthew 1:20-21
²⁰ But after he had considered this, an angel of the Lord appeared to him in a dream and said, "Joseph son of David, do not be afraid to take Mary home as your wife, because what is conceived in her is from the Holy Spirit."

I don't think anything makes God smile as much as us making a plan. He knew, I believe, that as soon as Joseph made his decision, Gabriel would once again go to work.

Why didn't God send Gabriel before Joseph had to go through all that turmoil?

How else would Joseph work out exactly how much he loved Mary? How much he was willing to sacrifice for that love? To understand he wasn't willing to sacrifice God in his life or the love he had for Mary.

And just when sleep was getting good … Life got gooder. (Did I mention I am from Mississippi? I know gooder isn't a word. Don't e-mail me over it, please. Ha!)

In this dream, the angel tells Joseph that everything Mary said was the truth. He basically gives him permission to take her home as his wife. The angel is working on behalf of God, as they are many times in the scripture. So, if the angel gave permission, who else gave Joseph permission. That's right, the one Joseph served and followed to the letter of the law, his God.

Mary had not cheated on him. The impossible becomes possible through truth and revelation.

Matthew 1:21
²¹" *"She will give birth to a son, and you are to give him the name Jesus, because he will save his people from their sins."*

Let me be clear here. What God did for me at Emmaus and Mary in the backyard, He also does for Joseph here in this dream.

Did you catch it?

Let me refresh your memory.

Gabriel to Mary: ³¹ *"You will conceive and give birth to a son, and you are to call him Jesus."* (Luke 1:31)

Gabriel to Joseph: ²¹ *"She will give birth to a son, and you are to give him the name Jesus."* (Matthew 1:21)

I would love to have been a fly on the wall when Mary and Joseph both blurted out that they had to name the baby Jesus. What a powerful "WOW GOD MOMENT" that would have been? What a testimony to what God brought them through and to.

Let's keep going... It's getting better than good. (Gooder?)

Matthew 1:24-25
²⁴ *When Joseph woke up, he did what the angel of the Lord had commanded him and took Mary home as his wife.* ²⁵ *But he did not consummate their marriage until she gave birth to a son. And he gave him the name Jesus.*

Reading this scripture only gives us a peek into life around Mary and Joseph after they come back together. They knew what God had done. They knew they were to be the parents of Gods one and only Son.

No one else in the whole town understood, though. One of the reactions of man (and woman) is to always believe the worse. Mary and Joseph were basically outcasts in their town, and the people around them believed the very worse about them, but they knew the truth.

I would image Mary's parents weren't 100% sure, but I bet they were so grateful to Joseph for staying with her. Even if they couldn't accept the truth, Joseph was a hero in their eyes. He took the higher road and spared the life of their little girl.

Regardless of what was going on around Mary and Joseph after he took her to be his bride, God provided a way out of Nazareth. And in a rather peculiar way... All because of a first-time census by the governor of Syria.

ON A ROAD TRIP

Remember I told you to mark your page in Luke? Well, I will give you a little time to stretch, then we will make our way back to the book of Luke.

Luke 2

The Birth of Jesus

2 In those days Caesar Augustus issued a decree that a census should be taken of the entire Roman world. ²(This was the first census that took place while[a] Quirinius was governor of Syria.) ³ And everyone went to their own town to register.

⁴ So Joseph also went up from the town of Nazareth in Galilee to Judea, to Bethlehem the town of David, because he belonged to the house and line of David. ⁵ He went there to register with Mary, who was pledged to be married to him and was expecting a child.

The story of the inn, stable, manger and the birth of the Savior of the world is known to millions of people. You don't have to be a Christian to know the story. But being a Christian, the story is heard from the heart and not the head. Christian or not, as you read the next few pages, your life can be changed if you open yourself up for love that pours out from a God that sent His only son so that you can have eternal life.

Let's pick up where we left off with Mary and Joseph in the town of Nazareth. As you can imagine, they are the gossip of the small town. Shunned by almost everyone. No more smiles and laughter from the town people when they walk by.

One of the things that has not changed much in our world from theirs is the judgment people pass on others when they only know a little of the truth.

As a pastor for the last fifteen years, I can assure you gossip and judgmental people are the two things that cripple a church faster than lack of money. God can deal very easily with the lack of money. Judgmental people that feel the need to be in charge push God out.

I believe it is one of the blessings God poured over Joseph and Mary. I know Jesus was prophesied to be born in Bethlehem, and the prophecy had to be fulfilled, but dig a little deeper with me here.

There is always an abundance of blessings around God's decisions. Getting out of Nazareth and the heart-hurting gossip was a side blessing for Joseph and Mary.

They might not have seen an eighty-mile journey with a nine-month pregnant Mary by foot and donkey as a blessing though. Joseph could have left Mary in Nazareth, but that was not God's design, was it?

Let's look at the Revdeb version of perhaps why God didn't let Joseph go it alone.

Sometimes it is better to not be in someone else's shoes, and this is one of those times for watching Joseph. He had a wife that he knew was carrying the Son of God. They had not heard from the angel since he last spoke to Joseph in a dream. Everything from then on was decisions Mary and Joseph made. No direction from God.

Do you ever feel that way?

"Where are you, God?"

"Which way do I go from here?"

"Show me the path, and I will gladly follow it."

And... silence.

Back to Joseph's mental battle. "Do I take Mary with me? She's nine months pregnant. This is at least an eighty-mile journey over very difficult roads. With the best of conditions, it would have taken at least four days to complete the journey."

Joseph knew it wasn't the best of conditions. But what were their other options? Mary's parents lived in Nazareth, and he knew he could leave her with them.

So, what was the problem with that decision?

Joseph could not protect her from the townspeople if he were gone. Remember, many of Joseph's *friends* believed they both had broken Jewish laws by consummating their marriage before the year was up.

If Joseph left her, she probably would have been taken by the "in charge – judgmental" people and stoned to death.

My favorite scenario? Mary standing up to Joseph and saying, "You are my husband. Where you go – I go."

We have a thirteen-year-old young woman, who had stood toe to toe with the angel, Gabriel when he told her that life as she knew it was over.

She looked him square in the eyes and said [38] *"I am the Lord's servant," Mary answered. "May your word to me be fulfilled." (Luke 1:38)*

She faced the townspeople, Joseph, and her parents and never backed down from declaring the truth of how the baby in her womb was conceived.

She proudly held her head high as she walked through the town of Nazareth with Joseph, never letting on how hurt she was from the cruel words of her people. A people that had loved her a few months prior.

There was no way she was letting Joseph leave her behind. That being settled, the bags were packed, the donkey prepared, and the first step to Bethlehem was taken.

~

A movie came out a few years ago called, *"The Nativity Story."* My granddaughter and I watch it many times during the Christmas season. The rest of the time we are watching Hallmark Christmas movies – yes – we are saps for romantic movies, and *"The Nativity Story"* is one of the greatest love story movies of all time.

A part in the movie that I love is the starting of the journey for Joseph and Mary as they leave Nazareth. The townspeople are out watching them leave, and they all have disgusted looks on their faces. Joseph turns to Mary (who is sitting on the donkey) and says, "I think they are going to miss us," with a huge smile on his face.

What a great response to such a hard situation. Bravo, Joseph.

The journey they were taking was not a trip they could ignore. Joseph could not just decide not to go. This was a mandatory trip proclaimed by the governor of Syria. Every Jewish man had to go to the home of his descendants and register in that town.

Joseph was a descendant in the line of David. David being from Bethlehem, meant that was where Joseph had to go to register.

I mentioned earlier in the book about love growing deeper and stronger by going through life together. Mary and Joseph only had each other as they took this long trip.

They were not alone physically because many people were traveling toward Jerusalem and Bethlehem to register. Most likely they joined a caravan of people. If nothing else, but for the protection it gave everyone from robbers.

They had seven or eight days of sharing a loaf of bread together at night by the campfire, seven or eight days of taking care of each other when no one else could. Can you hear the conversations they shared under the stars? The same stars God placed in the sky.

"What if I am not good enough?"

"What do you teach the child that belongs to the God of all creation?"

Do you feel Joseph's concerns? He is a carpenter, a simple woodworker.

I know there are times in your life you felt inadequate for the job before you, but how do you think Joseph must have felt when the night was quiet, and the stars in the sky seemed to haunt him? God had chosen him to love and care for Mary. The fine print at the end of the contract said, "oh, and just FYI Joseph, the woman you love and are in charge of protecting, is the woman God chose to carry the Savior of the world. Until His time comes, YOU are the one to teach him, protect him, and love him."

Sign and date, please.

Back to the journey…

Let's look at one more thing before we get to the town of Bethlehem. Once again, slip on the sandals of Joseph and make sure you strap yourself in tight.

It is the moment he steps on the top of the hill, and his precious town of Jerusalem comes into view. How his heart swelled to be looking down on a city that many had fought, died, and suffered for.

His thoughts had to return to the child in Mary's womb. If he could have imagined the highest thoughts, it would not have come close to what Jesus was going to do for this town and all mankind.

They would have traveled right through the streets of Jerusalem to get to the city of Bethlehem. Bethlehem is five miles from Jerusalem.

Over the last few days, Mary had begun to feel labor pains. As she looked at Joseph with love and admiration, she sees how tired he is and what a great burden he carries on his shoulders. She knew he would never complain though. Maybe the pains were just from sitting too long. She would feel better once they reached Bethlehem, and she could finally get a good night's rest.

The closer to Bethlehem, the harder the pain. She knew she would not be able to hide it from Joseph much longer. The baby must be coming.

Luke 2:6-7

⁶ While they were there, the time came for the baby to be born, ⁷ and she gave birth to her firstborn, a son. She wrapped him in cloths and placed him in a manger, because there was no guest room available for them.

The town of Bethlehem was packed with visitors. The ancestral line of David was massive.

Back to Revdeb version!

Joseph was feeling so much weight lifted off his shoulders as they stepped across the border into Bethlehem. All in all, it had been a great trip. Mary was safe and never complained at all. Nothing happened that could not be handled by the two of them together.

His love for Mary had grown every day as they talked about what life would be like for them when they returned to Nazareth. They dreamed plans. She laughed at his jokes and calmed his worries about their future.

Joseph was loving the peace that surrounded him until it was all broken by the loud cry of pain from Mary.

He knew the moment he saw her face that he should have recognized it sooner. He caught her a few times, the last two days, looking like she was in pain. She had always assured him it was just from the journey, but now he knew that she was in labor.

Thank goodness. They had finally made it to Bethlehem. Joseph headed toward the first inn.

No room.

The next inn.

No room.

Mary was in more and more pain. The Inn Keeper assured him that he would find no room in the town of Bethlehem.

The Census that brought Mary and Joseph to Bethlehem also brought many others that were already occupying the rooms.

The last innkeeper had a stable out back where they could at least be safe for the night. They would be among the animals there, but it was the best he could do for them.

The baby was close to being delivered, so Joseph and Mary took what was offered and made a place for Mary to deliver God's son.

God and Joseph shared that first moment of life for Jesus. God breathed the breath of life into his son's lungs, just as he did thousands of years before when Adam took his first breath.

Joseph shared in the moment by being the hands that helped Jesus come into this world. The first hands that held Jesus belonged to the man God picked out to be the earthly father of his eternal son.

That, my friends, should put all of us in a place of awe!

As Mary and Joseph held their newborn baby, they began to hear a noise outside the stable. Joseph took a stance in front of Mary and Jesus to protect them from whatever was making their way toward the opening of the stable.

THE ARRIVAL OF GUESTS

L et's pick back up in Scripture.

Luke 2:
⁸ And there were shepherds living out in the fields nearby, keeping watch over their flocks at night. ⁹ An angel of the Lord appeared to them, and the glory of the Lord shone around them, and they were terrified.

¹⁰ But the angel said to them, "Do not be afraid. I bring you good news that will cause great joy for all the people. ¹¹ Today in the town of David a Savior has been born to you; he is the Messiah, the Lord. ¹² This will be a sign to you: You will find a baby wrapped in cloths and lying in a manger."

¹³ Suddenly a great company of the heavenly host appeared with the angel, praising God and saying, ¹⁴ "Glory to God in the highest heaven, and on earth peace to those on whom his favor rests."

The hillside between Jerusalem and Bethlehem was a great place for shepherds to take their sheep. At night, the shepherds would get the sheep to lay down, and many of the shepherds would sit together under the stars and share stories handed down to them for years.

That night would change the stories the shepherds told forever. God had chosen only one group of people to proclaim, in the most glorious way, that His Son, the Savior of the World, was born.

That group of people were the lowest on the economic totem pole in those days. It is no wonder that scripture said they were terrified.

Let's head up to the mountain and watch the wonder together...

There they were, the shepherds, trying to outdo each other during storytelling time. When suddenly, the sky lit up as if it were high noon instead of the darkest time of night.

Before they could even begin to figure out why, an Angel of the Lord appeared in all his splendor. It had to have been a wonder to behold. The problem the shepherds had with it, was their own self-worth. They knew in this world they were nobodies. If an Angel appeared and the sky lit up like the noonday sun, it could only mean one thing for them – death.

The Angel quickly recognizes the fear on the faces of the shepherds. He does not let them live in that fear for any time. What he must share with them is a Joy that goes way beyond any fear.

Luke 2: 10

10 But the angel said to them, "Do not be afraid. I bring you good news that will cause great joy for all the people."

The angel lets them know very quickly that the news he is bringing them is not fearful, but of great joy for all the people. I think just the sight of the heavens opening would still have some of the shepherds cowering in fear and missing the "for all people" part.

Luke 2:11
¹¹ "Today in the town of David a Savior has been born to you; he is the Messiah, the Lord."

Throughout the entire Christmas story, this verse is my favorite. If you read it in a rush, you miss the most important part of the story. The angel is letting the shepherds know that the Savior, the Messiah, has been born in the city of David.

The entire message of the Angel on the hilltop, the story of John, Zechariah, and Elizabeth, the road trip to Bethlehem, all comes down to this one statement. These two little words that so many people don't understand today, any more than the shepherds did over two-thousand years ago.

That day, in the town of David, a Savior was born ----- **TO YOU!**

~

Luke 2:12
¹² "This will be a sign to you: You will find a baby wrapped in cloths and lying in a manger."

I am hoping from reading this scripture, you are starting to see a pattern of how God gives you information so you can believe the unbelievable.

Revdeb version:

Now, head on down the hill, take a right at the third rock on the left and look for the stable with this huge light shining overhead. Be careful of the dude standing over the woman and baby, he is very protective.

Look inside and *"You will find a baby wrapped in cloths and lying in a manger."*

Here's your sign. Bill Engvall has nothing on the angels.

Luke 2:15-20
¹⁵ When the angels had left them and gone into heaven, the shepherds said to one another, "Let's go to Bethlehem and see this thing that has happened, which the Lord has told us about."
¹⁶ So they hurried off and found Mary and Joseph, and the baby, who was lying in the manger. ¹⁷ When they had seen him, they spread the word concerning what had been told them about this child, ¹⁸ and all who heard it were amazed at what the shepherds said to them. ¹⁹ But Mary treasured up all these things and pondered them in her heart. ²⁰ The shepherds returned, glorifying and praising God for all the things they had heard and seen, which were just as they had been told.

It might have taken a few minutes to grasp the reality of what just took place, but the shepherds all agreed to head off to Bethlehem to check it out.

¹⁶ They found Mary, Joseph and Jesus just as the Angel had told them they would. They left there, glorifying and praising God for everything they had seen and heard.

I gain great joy at the shepherds being the ones God proclaimed his Son's birth to first. The reason is because I believe if I were born in that time, I would have been as lowly as a shepherd. I would have been one of the ones to first see the Savior of the World.

And just like the shepherds then and all of us today, you cannot encounter the savior without wanting to sing, shout, and glorify the Lord.

This basically ends the Christmas Story. I realize some of you, if not all, are wondering where The Wise Men are. Where is King Herod, the evil king in all of this?

In the Biblical story, the wise men did not come to the stable. This was a man-made story. A good one, but not the biblically correct one. The wise men came about two years after the birth of Jesus, and their story is celebrated during Epiphany, sometime around January 6th in most churches.

When King Herod ordered the death of all the babies in Bethlehem, remember the age he ordered killed. Children two and under. Now, don't go remove your wise men from your Nativity scenes. Enjoy the beauty of the manger scene in its fullness. Just know the whole story is a little more spread out than maybe you realized.

I believe one of the reasons we add them to the manger scene is if not, their story may get lost in the scriptures. The story of their journey, the gifts they brought, and the worship they did over Jesus, adds to the certainty of the baby being the Son of God.

Before I close, we must head back over to the hills of Judea and enter the living room of Zechariah and Elizabeth on the eighth day after the birth of John.

Luke 2:57-60

⁵⁷ When it was time for Elizabeth to have her baby, she gave birth to a son. ⁵⁸ Her neighbors and relatives heard that the Lord had shown her great mercy, and they shared her joy.

⁵⁹ On the eighth day they came to circumcise the child, and they were going to name him after his father Zechariah, ⁶⁰ but his mother spoke up and said, "No! He is to be called John."

Please remember as we head back to Elizabeth's home, that John is about six months older than Jesus. It is a custom in the Jewish religion to not name your child until the eighth day when they are circumcised.

It is a huge family event. A time of great celebration for the family, and in this scripture, many of the family has gathered for the occasion.

Everyone had so much excitement and were ready to place Zechariah's only son with his Father's name. If you recall from the beginning of the Christmas story, Zechariah was given very specific instructions about his child.

Let me remind you.

Luke 1

¹³ But the angel said to him: "Do not be afraid, Zechariah; your prayer has been heard. Your wife Elizabeth will bear you a son, and you are to call him John.

¹⁴ He will be a joy and delight to you, and many will rejoice because of his birth, ¹⁵ for he will be great in the sight of the Lord. He is never to take wine or other fermented drink, and he will be filled with the Holy Spirit even before he is born.

¹⁶ He will bring back many of the people of Israel to the Lord their God. ¹⁷ And he will go on before the Lord, in the spirit and power of Elijah, to turn the hearts of the parents to their children and the disobedient to the wisdom of the righteous—to make ready a people prepared for the Lord."

Among many other things about the child Zechariah and Elizabeth would soon be having, the most important was the name.

13b "You are to call him John."

There were probably plenty of hand signs and written confirmation between Elizabeth and Zechariah the nine months they were waiting for the birth of their son.

One of them would have been in deep discussion on the name that they were told to name the baby. I doubt either one of them fussed about it. They were both so in awe of what God had done for them that they would have named him Skeeter if that was the name Gabriel told them. Thank the good Lord it wasn't Skeeter.

Back to the house.

Elizabeth has spoken above the noise of the family and said, *"No! He is to be called John."*

Even if you have very little imagination, you can come up with the looks on the old auntie's faces when Elizabeth made this statement. Remember, Zechariah might have been getting very good at sign language by then, but he still couldn't speak.

Luke 1:61

61 They said to her, "There is no one among your relatives who has that name."

Hands on hips. Mouths open in shock. "Why I never," coming from Uncle Jim Bob. (Roll with me on this one...) "How do you dare not name him after his father? It's custom!"

Here is my favorite part. The "relatives" decide Elizabeth has lost

51

her ever-loving marbles and no longer speak to her. They go over her head.

Luke 1:62

⁶² Then they made signs to his father, to find out what he would like to name the child.

I love this. They made signs to his father. I am grateful Elizabeth is a good God loving/fearing woman. I am afraid I would have been making signs back at them!

Zechariah is a devoted and loving husband.

Luke 1:63

⁶³ He asked for a writing tablet, and to everyone's astonishment he wrote, "His name is John."

Don't miss the wink between husband and wife. Don't miss the smirk of a smile on the lips of Elizabeth.

Luke 1:64

⁶⁴ Immediately his mouth was opened and his tongue set free, and he began to speak, praising God.

How about that! Gabriel made good on his word. As if we expected anything different.

Luke 1:20

²⁰⁾ "And "now you will be silent and not able to speak until the day this happens, because you did not believe my words, which will come true at their appointed time."

I like to think Zechariah's first spoken words were, "Alright, all of you, OUT!"

But maybe that's just my humanity talking... It rears up sometimes, as I'm sure yours does too.

I hope you enjoyed the Christmas story verse by verse. I loved each and every word in this story and have spent many Christmases telling it from my pulpit.

It's a journey worth studying, remembering, and dwelling on. It's their story; it's our story; it's everyone's story. Christ came for all of us, leaving none out. This is the beginning of the tale, and we know where it ends, but for now... let's leave the room filled with wonder, the angel's in the air, and a simple carpenter and his wife sharing the greatest moment in all of History.

For unto **YOU** a child is born...

Merry Christmas,
    Pastor Deb

MY FAVORITE CHRISTMAS
CHILDREN'S MESSAGE

(Unknown author)

The Legend of the Silver Ice Tinsels

The night was cold, and the noise from town told the little spider in the cave that something was going on. It was better to stay back in the cave than to venture out tonight.

It wasn't long before a young couple and a tiny baby came into the cave. They sure looked scared and cold.

"We will have to hide out here tonight Mary," the young man said.

"How will we be safe with all the soldiers looking for us?" the woman asked.

"You get some sleep, and I will keep watch," said the man.

They cuddled together in the back of my cave trying to stay warm. I noticed it wasn't long before all of them were asleep.

The little spider crawled down to get a closer look at the baby.

He thought to himself, "I wish there was something I could do." The spider then realized he could do something.

He went to the entrance to the cave and began to weave a web. He kept it up until the cave was completely covered in the web. At least they can be warm, the spider thought.

The next morning, you could hear the soldiers riding throughout the land. They came next to the cave and dismounted. The leader told them to check every cave. "Do not leave any unchecked." As a solider came near the cave with Mary, Joseph and baby Jesus in it, the leader told him not to bother with checking that cave.

"Why?" asked the soldier. The leader said, "That cave has not been disturbed. Look at the spiderweb. If someone had entered the cave, it would have been broken. Check the others."

That is the legend of why we add silver ice tinsels to our tree. It is to remind us even the smallest of us can make a huge difference for God.

BREATH OF HEAVEN

Mary's Song – Written by Chris Eaton
https://www.youtube.com/watch?v=TOQRtYYERGo

I have traveled many moonless nights
    Cold and weary with a babe inside
    And I wonder what I've done
    Holy Father, You have come
    And chosen me now to carry Your Son

I am waiting in a silent prayer
    I am frightened by the load I bear
    In a world as cold as stone
    Must I walk this path alone?
    Be with me now, be with me now

Breath of Heaven, hold me together

Be forever near me, breath of Heaven
Breath of Heaven, lighten my darkness
Pour over me Your holiness for You are holy
Breath of Heaven

Do you wonder as you watch my face
    If a wiser one should have had my place?
    But I offer all I am
    For the mercy of Your plan
    Help me be strong, help me be, help me

Breath of Heaven, hold me together
    Be forever near me, breath of Heaven
    Breath of Heaven, lighten my darkness
    Pour over me Your holiness for You are holy

Breath of Heaven, hold me together
    Be forever near me, breath of Heaven
    Breath of Heaven, lighten my darkness
    Pour over me Your holiness for You are holy
    Breath of Heaven, breath of Heaven
    Breath of Heaven

JOSEPH'S LULLABY

Written by: Bart Millard
https://www.youtube.com/watch?v=9ehZ5s_icFE

Go to sleep my Son
    This manger for your bed
    You have a long road before You
    Rest Your little head

Can You feel the weight of Your glory?
    Do You understand the price?
    Or does the Father guard Your heart for now
    So You can sleep tonight?

Go to sleep my Son
    Go and chase Your dreams
    This world can wait for one more moment

Go and sleep in peace

I believe the glory of Heaven
    Is lying in my arms tonight
    But Lord, I ask that He for just this moment
    Simply be my child

Go to sleep my Son
    Baby, close Your eyes
    Soon enough You'll save the day
    But for now, dear Child of mine
    Oh my Jesus, Sleep tight

AUTHOR'S NOTE

I so enjoyed sharing my view of the Christmas story with you. I hope you join me on this new journey God has me on. I'll be working on the book of Esther next, as it's one of my favorites. Make sure you follow me on Amazon if you're interested in seeing when something new is released.

You can also keep up with me on my blog – Raindrops by Rev Deb.

Thanks for picking up a copy of *Journey to Bethlehem*. I hope it touched your heart, opened your eyes, or at least brought you into the Christmas mood a little more.

May God be glorified through it, and may you be blessed.

ABOUT THE AUTHOR

REVEREND DEBBIE DROST

In June of 2002, God called me into ministry. It was six years later, in May of 2010 that God asked me to step out of the mainstream denominational church and begin a new church for him.

My conversation with God began the same way Moses's did thousands of years ago on Mount Horeb, *"take your shoes off little girl,"* (Revdeb version) and ended with me repeating everything Moses said when God asked him to set the Israelites free.

I am not worthy. I am not as educated as so many others. What if I preach something wrong?

God told me something then, that has grown into a passion for me. He said "Just tell the story. Stick to my word, and you will be fine."

Those words, "Just tell the story," have led me down a path that has brought myself and others closer to Jesus.

From these stories and the love God has for this Mississippi barefoot pastor, the "Revdeb version" was born.

Made in the USA
Middletown, DE
28 August 2018